SCOTLAND

Text:	**Bill Harris**
Captions:	**Ros Cocks**
Design:	**Teddy Hartshorn**
Photography:	**Ronald W. Weir Photography, Pitlochry, Scotland**
	Andy Williams Photo Library, Guildford, England
	The Scottish Highland Photo Library, Inver-Gordon, Scotland
Editorial:	**Laura Potts**
Production:	**Ruth Arthur**
	Sally Connolly
	Neil Randles
	Jonathan Tickner
Director of Production:	**Gerald Hughes**

CLB 3475

© 1994 CLB Publishing, Godalming, Surrey, England.
All rights reserved.
Colour separation by Advance Laser, Hong Kong
Printed and bound by Poligrafici Calderara S.p.A., Italy
ISBN 1-85833-278-8

SCOTLAND

CLB
Colour Library Books

SCOTLAND

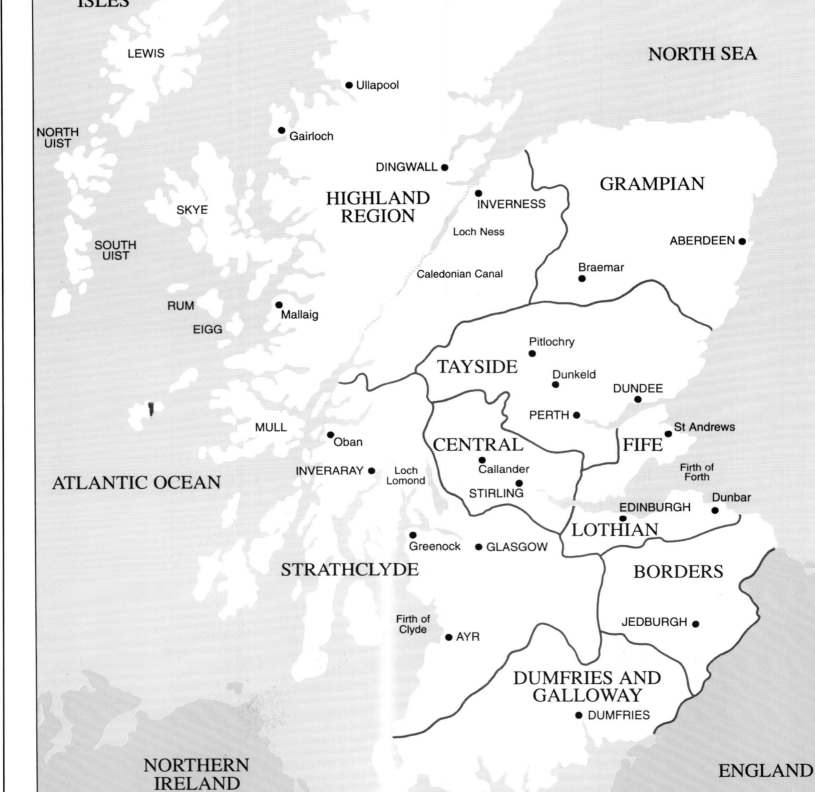

THE SHETLANDS

THE ORKNEYS

THE WESTERN ISLES

NORTH SEA

LEWIS

NORTH UIST

SKYE

SOUTH UIST

RUM

EIGG

MULL

ATLANTIC OCEAN

John O' Groats

Durness

Tongue

Ullapool

Gairloch

DINGWALL

HIGHLAND REGION

INVERNESS

Loch Ness

Caledonian Canal

GRAMPIAN

ABERDEEN

Braemar

Mallaig

Pitlochry

TAYSIDE

Dunkeld

DUNDEE

PERTH

St Andrews

Oban

CENTRAL

FIFE

INVERARAY

Loch Lomond

Callander

Firth of Forth

STIRLING

EDINBURGH

Dunbar

LOTHIAN

Greenock

GLASGOW

STRATHCLYDE

BORDERS

JEDBURGH

Firth of Clyde

AYR

DUMFRIES AND GALLOWAY

DUMFRIES

NORTHERN IRELAND

ENGLAND

CONTENTS

Fountain and castle,
Edinburgh, Lothian.

There are dozens of symbols of Scottishness. The tartan, the kilt, the bagpipe, the bonnet, a sprig of heather and an eagle's feather begin the long list. But you're not very likely to see any of those things on the underground in Glasgow, in an Edinburgh traffic jam or even at Inverness, the capital of the Highlands, where such things were once quite common. Of course, you'll see such traditional Scottish symbols at the hundreds of festivals that take place all over the country throughout the year, but don't be surprised if some of the costumes smell a little of mothballs, and the eagle feather is imported. The golden eagle, itself a symbol of the country's spirit, and the largest bird in all the British Isles, is almost extinct in Scotland. But then, some might say, so is the Scottish race.

At last count, Scotland's population was less than five million, but there are more than five times that many Scots living around the world in such places as Nova Scotia in Canada, Perth in Australia, Berwick in Pennsylvania. There is almost no place on earth that doesn't have Stewarts and Malcolms, MacDonalds or MacKenzies in its telephone directories, often in its list of prominent citizens. Indeed, Neil Armstrong, the first man on the moon, was a Scot. Of course, he went there as an American, but like many others of Scots ancestry, you can be sure that his heart was very much in the Highlands.

Armstrong's ancestors would have been surprised if they had known. This Highland thing is of fairly recent vintage as Scottish history goes. Robert Burns started the ball rolling in the late eighteenth century when he echoed the feelings of Scottish expatriates with the words: 'My heart's in the Highlands, my heart is not here;/ My heart's in the Highlands a-chasing the deer.' The same sentiments were expressed by Sir Walter Scott in the nineteenth century in his novel Waverley, the book that changed the world's view of Scotland in general and the Highlands in particular.

In the days before Burns and Scott bared their hearts and Scotland's soul to the world in general, the division between the country's Highlands and Lowlands was as distinct in their culture as in their geography. The border that separates them is a natural fault line running along a west to east diagonal from Dumbarton, north of Glasgow, to Stonehaven on the North Sea just south of Aberdeen. There are hills and mountains south of

the line, but they are usually classified as 'uplands', not to be confused with the Grampian and Northwest Highlands above it. From the earliest times, however, the real difference was in the people and, make no mistake, their hearts were not entwined.

A fourteenth-century version of what we might today call a sociologist noted that Scotland's coastal people were ' ... of civilized habits, trusty, patient and urbane, decent in their attire, affable and peaceful.' Their countrymen up in the mountains, on the other hand, were, in his opinion, ' ... savage and untamed, rude and independent', not to mention 'exceedingly cruel' and 'unsightly in dress'. This last comment referred to tartans, kilts and bonnets, and although his thoughts on the specifics of their outlandish costumes went unrecorded, the writer also probably had quite a few unkind words to describe bagpipes, which undoubtedly cropped up in conversations over wee drams of whisky alongside peat fires in the company of his kinsmen, quite obviously Lowlanders.

But it didn't really matter what he said or wrote because the Highlands and the Lowlands were further separated by a language barrier. In the south the language was Scots, which strongly resembled the English of Geoffrey Chaucer, but in the north and west Gaelic was spoken. The Gaelic language was imported, with some modifications, along with the Celts, who had moved across from central Europe to settle in Gaul and Britain centuries before.

Today, much of this conflict is forgotten and there is hardly anyone anywhere in the world with even a drop of Scottish blood in their veins who wouldn't consider Highland ways part of their heritage. Even though it represents a traditional minority in the culture, the romance of the Highlands is undeniable. All it takes is a little bit of imagination. Scotland itself does the rest. Almost no country in the world has as much living, breathing history at hand and few have a history quite as lively.

It is a history that goes back some 6,000 years, to an antiquity as old as the first glimmerings of civilization in the ancient Near East. The difference, of course, is that the Stone Age and Bronze Age people of the northern stretches of the British Isles never learned how to put their history in writing. They did, however, leave some clues about their presence and their skills in building, and some believe that human life first appeared in Britain up in the far north. There is an ancient, multi-chambered tomb at Maes Howe on the island of Orkney, for instance, that dates back to at least 2700 bc, about the same time the Egyptians began working on their great pyramids. Also on the island are the remains of the even older Stone Age settlement of Skara Brae, a collection of stone houses that were connected to one another by covered passageways. The island also boasts the Ring of Brodgar, a circle of stones precisely spaced and surrounded by a wide moat, nine feet deep, that was cut from solid rock as early as 1560 bc, roughly the same time Moses was leading his people out of Egypt. The Circle of Callanish, on the island of Lewis, in the Outer Hebrides, is similar to, though even older than, the famous stone circles at Stonehenge and Avebury in England, and every bit as beautiful and mysterious.

In comparatively recent times, probably about the seventh century bc, Celtic tribes began moving in and taking charge. It seems possible that they didn't take over without a fight, because there are hundreds of circular stone towers, called brochs, at the edges of fields in the far north and on the islands, obviously built for defence, although no one knows who built them, nor from whom they were defending themselves. In the west and south, hilltop forts sprang up wherever there was a hill worth holding, and it seems reasonable to assume that different tribes were at war with one another, a conclusion reflected in the clan wars of later history. Farms in those days were protected by stone walls, known as duns, and the houses of the people who worked the farms were sod huts, called weems, built over subterranean tunnels that served both for storage and for refuge. The really cautious lived in crannogs, islands built of logs in the centre of lakes like beaver lodges. The only way to reach them was across an ingenious wooden roadway a few inches under the water, making a sudden, sweeping attack virtually impossible. Exactly who it was that might have attacked, it is impossible to know. The recorded history of Scotland doesn't begin until ad 81. All the rest is educated guesswork.

The tale begins with the Roman conquest of Britain some forty years earlier. The annexation and civilization of the Britain was, in true Roman fashion, slow but steady, and after occupying the lowlands of England the legions pushed inexorably north and west, conquering Wales and the territory south of the Tyne known to them as Brigantia. Next on the list was the land they knew as Caledonia, the wilderness to the far north, and an army 20,000 strong led by Gnaeus Julius Agricola marched in that direction, assuming from past experience that the Caledonians would melt before them. They were wrong.

Agricola received his first set-back when his camp was attacked by surprise at night. A master tactician, he managed to counterattack from the rear and sent the Caledonians into retreat. The next day the two armies met in battle on the hillside that the Roman historian Tacitus – coincidentally Agricola's

Plockton and Loch Carron, Highland Region.

*Applecross Mountains and
the pass to Loch Kishorn,
Highland Region.*

son-in-law – called Mons Graupius. The Romans won the battle, but the war had just begun. It wasn't possible to secure the victory by following the defenders into the wild country they called home, and the Romans put off their fight for another day. By a quirk of fate, as Agricola was constructing of a fortress in the north in preparation for a new campaign, he and many of his legionaries were recalled to mainland Europe to defend the Empire. In the meantime the Caledonians were building forts, too, and within another three decades they had reduced the Roman presence to a handful. Then, when the experienced Ninth Legion marched north to tip the balance back in their favour, it was wiped out to the last man. At least, that's what historians believe. There is no record of a battle, no sign of a battleground. The Ninth Legion, 4,000 to 6,000 strong, simply vanished from the face of the earth.

Tacitus sounded a warning that such a thing might happen in his description of the Battle of Mons Graupius, in which he said Calgacus, a farmer who had become a soldier, rallied his people with oratory worthy of the Roman Senate. Whether such a man ever existed is still open to debate, even though he is the first man of Scotland to be remembered with a name, but the words Tacitus put in his mouth summed up the attitude of the people in a way that no amount of fighting ever could.

'Here at the world's end, on its last inch of liberty, we have lived unmolested to this day,' Calgacus allegedly said. ' … There are no other tribes to come; nothing but sea and cliffs, and these more deadly Romans whose arrogance you cannot escape by obedience and self-restraint. … If their enemy have wealth, they have greed; if he be poor, they are ambitious. … To plunder, butcher, steal, these things they misname empire; where they make a desert, they call it peace.'

After the loss of the Ninth Legion, the Emperor Hadrian decided that the Empire could easily survive without Caledonians among its subjects, and he ordered the construction of a fortified stone wall running seventy miles from sea to sea between the Tyne River and the Solway Firth to keep them in their place. Parts of the wall are still there, but the frontier it created, never quite secure, lasted just ten years, four years longer than it took to build it, before the new Emperor, Antoninus Pius, decided to move deeper into enemy territory. The resulting Antonine Wall, stretching between the Forth and the Clyde, was even less effective. By the end of the fourth century the Romans, who had even bigger troubles at home, gave up on Scotland and went away without leaving much behind except a couple of straight roads and a pair of walls they themselves would have preferred to forget.

In the two centuries following the Roman departure from Britain, Scotland came to be occupied by four principal peoples. The native Britons, displaced by invading Teutons, occupied western Scotland, as well as parts of Cumbria and Wales. Their new neighbours included the powerful Picts, who dominated the area from the Forth to Caithness, and the

*Laggan, Loch Laggan and
the Mamore Mountains,
Highland Region.*

Angles, occupying the lands north of the River Humber to the Firth of Forth. The Scots, who had migrated from Northern Ireland, occupied a kingdom they called Dalriada in the southwest. Although they were all, like the Britons themselves, of Celtic origin, they weren't kissing cousins, and if the blood in their veins was similar, it never made them think twice about spilling it. But soon, after a century or two, they had a new bond of sorts after Christianity arrived in the north.

There is some evidence that Christianity first arrived with the Roman soldiers, but missionary work proper seems to have been begun by St Ninian, who established a monastery at Whithorn in his native Strathclyde in ad 398, about thirty years after the Romans gave up on Scotland. His followers had some impact on the Picts and the Britons, but the Scots, who took their inspiration from Ireland, waited for more than a century and a half before the Word of God reached them through St Columba, who established a mission on the island of Iona in 563. He not only brought Christianity to the mainland Scots, but gave a new lease to their pride, which had recently been mauled by a crushing defeat at the hands of the Picts. Their king had died in battle and Columba, who was of royal birth himself, managed to have him replaced by a man of a stronger line, a choice that assured future dominance, or at least parity, over the Picts. But, in true Christian fashion, even though the Picts were enemies, Columba ventured north into their territory to convert them to his religion. It was there that he

gave credence to Scotland's most enduring legend.

The Picts were pagan, and as such witchcraft and magic played an important part in their lives. Such things gave power to their priests and they didn't take too kindly to the idea of a new religion in their midst, especially considering that the bearer of the gift had friends in high places back in Dalriada. Columba, however, confounded them with a contest of magic at the court of their king, and mystified them by sailing away against the wind. If that wasn't enough, he further impressed the king's subjects by subduing a sea serpent in Loch Less with no other weapon than the sign of the cross, and then informed the people that the monster was in his power and that his religion was their only protection against it. After that day, Christian monasteries sprang up all over the land of the Picts.

By the end of the seventh century all of the kingdoms were in the Christian fold, but they still weren't united. And their church wasn't in tune with Rome. Eventually the religious differences were settled, but the political differences persisted until a new enemy, Viking raiders from the north, landed in their midst. The invasion started slowly at first, but by the end of the ninth century the Vikings had become the virtual masters of Scotland. Their depredations were more damaging to the Picts than to any of the other peoples, and that opened an opportunity for Kenneth MacAlpin, King of the Scots, to declare himself ruler of all the territory north of the Forth. From that moment on, nothing more was heard of the Picts, who had ruled that land for more than a thousand years.

MacAlpin tried to force the Angles of Lothian – the area between the Tweed and Forth rivers – into his kingdom, but neither he nor his immediate successors were able to do it. It was not until 1018, following Malcolm II's victory in battle, that these lands were incorporated into the kingdom, and a unified Scottish state began to emerge. At the same time, the king of the Britons died without an heir, leaving his throne to be claimed by Malcolm's grandson, Duncan, who ruled over a kingdom that extended far to the south of the present Scottish border, until his death at the hands of Macbeth.

Macbeth, the central character is Shakespeare's play of the same name, may be remembered as one of the greatest villains of all time but the fact seems to be that the former Earl of Moray was an enlightened monarch during his seventeen years in power. Yet even if the people were happy, Duncan's son, Malcolm, who was in exile in England, was not. In 1054 he crossed the border with an English army to reclaim the throne and, after defeating Macbeth at Lumphanan, avenged his father three years later by dispatching the man he considered a pretender. Then, after killing the son of Macbeth's wife and so eliminating the only other rival claimant, Malcolm III became the undisputed King of Scotland. It was the English, however, who had helped him, and neither he nor his descendants were able to forget it.

In 1096, Malcolm married Margaret. Like Malcolm, Margaret had spent many years at the court of Edward the Confessor in England, and she began to change things to conform with her English ways. These changes dramatically altered Scottish life, from that of the clergy to the court nobles to ordinary people. Though the changes suited the Anglo-Saxons of the Lowlands, whose lifestyle required only minor adjustments, the Celts, up in the north, were muttering to themselves about the injustice of it all.

After Malcolm was killed in a battle against the Normans, he was succeeded by his uncle, Donald Bane, by then more than sixty years old. After a long exile in the Hebrides, he had become more Celtic than Saxon, and the English king sent Malcolm's son, Duncan, to depose the old man and get anglicisation back on track. He was successful, but was then murdered for his trouble, and Donald resumed his rule until an English army drove him into exile again and replaced him with the friendlier Edgar, Duncan's half brother. The confusion was further confounded when Edgar died and was succeeded by his brother Alexander, who wasn't really interested in the job, allowing anarchy to settle in the territory north of the River Spey and giving control of the lands south of the Forth to another brother named David. If it all conspired to make the people of Scotland feel like second class citizens of England, Alexander managed to rub it in by marrying the daughter of England's King Henry I, who himself just happened to be married to Alexander's sister, Maud. This made Alexander Henry's son-in-law and his brother-in-law at the same time. The feeling among many of his subjects was that England was sleeping in Scotland's bed, and it made them very uncomfortable indeed.

The situation didn't improve much when Alexander died and his brother David, who was already the ruler of southern Scotland, became king. Like his brothers, he had been raised in England, and through marriage he had become the Earl of both Huntington and Northampton, each in its own right a source of great power in England, and, like his late brother, was the king's brother-in-law. Using his new power, he lavished great estates on his Norman friends, and over time the aristocracy, at least in the Lowlands, became almost all French-speaking. To his credit, David did manage to bring some benefits to the Scottish people, but there were large pockets of people, especially in the north, who would have none of it. People in the islands as well as much of the Highlands routinely ignored their king and, apart from their loyalty to their own clan chiefs, recognised no higher authority than the King of Norway.

The situation changed dramatically after David died and Norway's monarch moved in to sack Aberdeen while his ally, the Lord of Argyll, destroyed Glasgow. With that, the English annexed Northumbria and the fat was in the fire. Scotland's new king, William, bent on revenge against the English, formed an alliance with France in 1165 and began plotting an invasion of England. The plot failed, some say by an act of God, when a sudden fog rolled in as the invasion forces moved south. William was captured after the debacle and banished to France, where he signed the Treaty of Falaise, which not only confirmed England's right to Northumbria, but put all of Scotland, including its church, firmly under the English thumb. It took the humiliated King William fifteen years to set things right when he made a deal, for what amounted to a king's ransom, with Richard the Lionheart to fund one of his crusades in exchange for his renunciation of the treaty.

William bought a peace with England that lasted more than a century, but no amount of money could buy off the chiefs in the north and the west, who continued thumbing their nose at the Scottish monarch. The King of Norway was a thorn in Scotland's side, too, until a peace treaty was sealed with the marriage of Alexander III's daughter, Margaret, to Eric of Norway. At the same time, Alexander himself secured English friendship by marrying the daughter of Henry III, also named Margaret. The marriage pact with Norway has held up to this day, but the love affair with England wasn't quite so long lasting.

After Alexander died, his granddaughter, the infant daughter of the King of Norway, was his only heir. It was too good an opportunity for England's Edward I to pass up and he suggested that the baby Queen should marry his son. A treaty was signed and a ship dispatched to carry the little girl to her destiny, but her destiny, as it happened, was an untimely death at sea.

With that, the Scottish throne was up for grabs and more than a dozen contenders reached out for it, a situation resolved, or so he thought, by Edward I, who went to Berwick Castle and announced that he had chosen John de Balliol, a noble of Norman background whose mother was a descendant of Duncan I, to be King of the Scots. Balliol was pleased, of course, but couldn't stomach the English king's demand that he should contribute men and money to help England launch an attack on France. He responded to the demands by repudiating his ties to Edward, forging an alliance with France – known as the Auld Alliance – and planning an attack on England.

Two days after the war began, Edward mounted a counterattack and quickly defeated Balliol, but not without the help of the Scottish nobles, most of whom were his vassals. Chief among them was Robert Bruce, whose claim to the throne was identical to Balliol's, but who, along with some two thousand other nobles, signed the 'Ragman's Roll', pledging homage to the English king and recognising him as the legitimate King of Scotland.

The nobles, however, had acquiesed under pressure and after a decade or so of resentful subservience, some of them began kicking over the traces, including another Robert Bruce, son of the Robert who had signed Edward's document. As a leader of what is sometimes called a heroic band of rebels and at other times a hotbed of self-serving treachery, young Bruce came out of the shadows in 1306 when he stabbed Red John Comyn, an outspoken supporter of Balliol, and left him to bleed to death in a church. The result was not only the start of a blood feud between the Bruces and the Comyns, but Robert's quick excommunication, the ultimate liability for a man who would be king.

But arrogance may be the ultimate asset of such a man, and Robert Bruce displayed one of history's great examples of it a few weeks after the murder by having himself crowned king, not once but twice in two days. Naturally, Edward responded by sending in an avenging army, and within days the new king's chief supporters had been hung, drawn and quartered. Isobel of Fife, the Countess of Buchan, who had placed the crown on Bruce's head, and Bruce's wife were imprisoned. Bruce himself managed to escape and, after a year of setbacks against the British forces, had gathered enough tough-minded allies to make Edward personally lead an army into Scotland to crush the rebels. The English king died soon afterward and his heir, Edward II, withdrew his army, leaving Bruce to his own devices. Bruce's idea of that was to subdue his enemies. Within fifteen years he had not only succeeded in that goal, but had driven the English from all of Scotland except Stirling and invaded England itself. It was then that Edward decided he ought to do something.

When his army arrived, it outnumbered Bruce's by about three to one, but Bruce had the strategic advantage. The battleground, thick marsh at Bannockburn, went a long way towards evening the odds, and within hours the English soldiers, with their king well ahead of them, were on the run in the general direction of England. The war lasted another fourteen years, but after Bannockburn all the fighting was outside Scotland, including battles in Ireland, where the grateful people made Robert Bruce's brother their king.

But the most grateful people of all were in Scotland. By the

Loch Awe and Kilchurn Castle, Strathclyde.

Eilean Donan Castle on Loch Duich at Dornie, Highland Region.

time he died, Robert Bruce had become the country's first bona fide national hero and his subjects were united as they never had been before.

Things began to unravel again when Bruce died and was succeeded by his five-year-old son and only heir, David II. Early in his reign, Scottish nobles who had been stripped of their estates for supporting the English against his father, engineered the elevation of Balliol's son, Edward, to the throne. Although other nobles sent him packing before he could get comfortable in his new position, young David himself was captured by the English and for a dozen years was a 'guest' in Edward's court. In the meantime, the regency in Scotland was entrusted to Robert Bruce's young grandson, Robert Stewart, and in 1371, when David died, he became Scotland's first Stewart king. He himself was succeeded by his son, Robert III, a sickly cripple who deferred to a string of regents to carry out his responsibilities. One of them was his uncle, the Duke of Albany, who Robert believed was determined to remove his heir, James, from succession. To ward off the threat, he sent his grandson, James, to the safety of France. Fate went against him, however, and the young man was captured by pirates and was turned over to the English, who held him hostage for eighteen years, during which time Robert died and Albany's power had dramatically increased. The nobles used the time to expand their estates and strengthen their private armies, and in the north the clan chiefs allied themselves with the English,

although none of them had any intention of relinquishing any of their personal power.

The situation began to change when the hostage king, James I, returned to Scotland. He had received a first-rate education during his years in exile and was well-prepared to assume his role as king. But no one could have been prepared for the anarchy and lawlessness he found. He began to break the power of the nobles by executing all of the Albany family and annexing their estates, and he gave the clan chiefs something to think about by arresting nearly forty of them. His determination and sweeping reforms served him, and Scotland, well, but it earned him quite a few enemies and he was murdered, leaving the throne to a six-year-old child, James II, and the government of the country to another regent.

The first of those regents was the hugely powerful Earl of Douglas. He might have managed eventually to become king himself, had he not died two years into his regency, leaving his estates and power to two teenage sons. As if to present a show of friendship, the new regent, Sir William Crichton, invited the lads to dinner with the boy king at Edinburgh Castle and then proceeded to murder them before the main course was served. Meanwhile, the eight-year-old king went right on playing with his food. It was the beginning of the end for the Douglases. After reaching maturity and taking control of his own affairs, James attempted to defuse an alliance among the Douglases, the equally powerful Crawfords and John, the self-styled King

*Buachaille Etive Mor and
waterfall, Glen Etive,
Highland Region.*

of the Isles, by extending the hand of friendship to the Earl of Douglas. When he was rebuffed, as was probably to be expected, he invited the Earl to Stirling Castle, where he stabbed him to death over dinner. Not a very hospitable act, to be sure, but the people supported their king and one of Douglas's important allies in the English Parliament announced that the Earl was 'guilty of his own death', as a consequence of his stubbornness in not accepting James's offer of friendship. Thus ended the power of the house that is still remembered as the 'Black Douglases'. Not long afterwards the murdered man's heirs were killed in battle and their allies, the Crawfords and John of the Isles, swore allegiance to the Crown and peace came to Scotland.

England was far from peaceful. After a crushing defeat in France, a test of wills emerged between the houses of York and Lancaster in the Wars of the Roses over the succession to the throne. James decided to wade into the conflict on the side of York and was killed for his trouble. It left Scotland with yet another boy king, nine-year-old James III.

When he was nineteen the young king married the daughter of the King of Norway, and Scotland received the islands of Orkney and Shetland as her dowry. James, although he expanded his country's territory, was no statesman, and because they perceived him as weak, not to mention the fact that he pointedly preferred the company of intellectuals, the nobles grew to despise him. Before long they rose up against him, hanged his favourites and elevated his son, James IV to the throne. The boy's father tried to fight back, but was mortally wounded in the battle that followed. When he asked for a priest to administer the last rites, the man who came forward killed him.

It was an important day for the nobles, including Archibald Douglas, scion of a branch of the infamous family, the 'Red Douglases', who was intent on restoring his family's name, if not its influence. He became an advisor to the fifteen-year-old James, along with members of other formerly-powerful families who were convinced that happy days were here again.

For his part, the young king wasn't at all happy about the circumstances that had raised him to the throne. As a sign of his remorse he carried an iron chain around his body for the rest of his life. But James IV wasn't ready to humble himself in any other way, least of all to the nobles whose power he respected in its own right, but not at the expense of his own. When civil war broke out again a year into his reign, he personally led his troops into battle, defeated the rebels and restored order in record time. Then he began to restore Scotland itself. It was during those years that the Renaissance reached Scotland, and with much thanks to James, thrived. His court was one of Europe's most brilliant and the country was enriched with scores of palaces and churches. For the first time, buildings were built of stone rather than wood, printing presses appeared, and with them expanded literacy. Trade with other countries increased, too, and there was prosperity in the land. What was happening in Edinburgh and the Lowlands, however, went largely unnoticed in the Highlands, where life

went on as it had for hundreds of years. Most of Scotland's kings had either been persuaded or had decided on their own to respect the status quo, but James IV elected to try to change things.

Among his other impressive accomplishments the king was a gifted linguist, conversant in several languages, including Gaelic, the one that had eluded his predecessors. Armed with this weapon, he ventured into the Highlands, an expedition prompted by a recent declaration of war against the king, and his own father, by Angus Og, son of John, Lord of the Isles. It had split the Western Highlands into two factions and began a long and bloody feud between the MacDonalds and their neighbours, the MacLeods and MacKenzies. James hoped to defuse the situation by encouraging the Highlanders to rechannel their energy into more useful pursuits. Yet, even though James could speak to the clan chiefs in their own language, he couldn't make his motives understood. His only alternative, he thought, was to revoke old charters and redivide the land, as well as authority over it, among feudal lords he could trust. The result was more uprisings, but the king, by increasing his military presence, managed to keep them contained and felt free to take on the problems of the rest of Europe.

With that in mind, he ordered the construction of the world's mightiest fleet of warships to sail against the Turks, who were marching toward Vienna and threatening all of Christendom. He cemented ties with England by marrying Margaret Tudor, the twelve-year-old daughter of Henry VII, and resurrected the Auld Alliance with France, putting himself in the position of peace-keeper between the two old enemies. Peace was threatened from beyond, however, and when the Pope's Holy League attacked France in 1511, England's King Henry VII felt honour-bound to get into the fight. His brother-in-law, the King of Scotland, thought otherwise and launched an attack on England, leading what many consider the best army Scotland ever saw. But it wasn't good enough. In the fighting that followed, James was killed, as was his son, a host of nobles, many Highland clan chiefs and the flower of Scotland's youth. It was a dark day for Scotland, made darker still by the fact that James V, the new king, was a babe in arms who had not yet taken his first step nor uttered his first word.

The regency was taken over by the baby's mother, Margaret Tudor, whose heart was most assuredly not in the Highlands. Although most of the nobility had been wiped out in the Battle of Flodden Edge, there were enough noblemen left to add a dash of intrigue to Scottish affairs. By the time the king was fourteen and considered mature enough to govern, he was a prisoner of the Douglases, who by then had taken the government into their own hands. James eventually managed to escape and banished his captors to England. Soon afterwards he found himself the centre of the attention of the entire Christian world, and his country the key to a struggle for influence in a world divided by the Reformation.

The fact that James was still unmarried was at the heart of the matter. The religious power brokers knew that his choice of a bride could determine whether Scotland would remain

Catholic or turn Protestant, and every king and emperor, even the Pope himself, came forward with appropriate young women for his consideration. James chose the daughter of the King of France, who died before the honeymoon was over, and then took Marie de Guise, another Frenchwoman, as his bride. When her two sons died, the religious establishment redoubled its efforts. The Catholics offered him more power by making him King of Ireland, and the Protestants, in the person of England's Henry VIII, brought their own power to bear with open threats. James responded by attacking England, but his people refused to support him and he was badly beaten. Adding to his despondency was the news that his wife had given birth to his heir and that the child was a girl. Less than a week later he was dead and the week-old Mary became Queen of Scots.

Henry VIII responded quickly by suggesting the marriage of his son, Edward, to the baby girl, but her mother, representing both Catholic and French interests, would have none of it and Henry decided to take Protestantism into Scotland by force. The atrocities, the burning and pillaging that followed were the worst Scotland has ever seen and, in some circles at least, hatred for the English hasn't cooled since.

The Protestant cause wasn't lost even if the despised Henry was its champion. Even the Pope himself was forced to admit that his Scottish bishops were corrupt, and the people knew that he didn't know, or wouldn't admit, the half of it. Although Scotland was officially Catholic and the Church owned half the wealth in the country, English translations of the Bible began appearing, in defiance of the law, and soon the popular movement against the Church began swelling to epidemic proportions.

A prime mover in the new thinking was a young priest named John Knox. After a forced exile to France, Knox found himself chaplain to England's Protestant king, Edward VI. Edward's death and Mary Tudor's accession saw the reintroduction of Catholicism to England and Knox went to Geneva. There he became a disciple of John Calvin, whose ideas were redefining the principles of Protestantism.

When he finally returned to Scotland, Knox found the Protestant movement in full swing. But the fifteen-year-old Queen Mary – who had just married the Dauphin of France, bringing the two countries closer together than ever – and her still-powerful mother were determined to nip the heresy in the bud. Knox added fuel to the fire with his impassioned sermons and his followers responded by attacking Catholic churches and smashing what they considered idolatrous images. In the meantime, Protestantism returned to England when Elizabeth succeeded Mary as queen, and if the Scots had no other rapport with the English, it seemed to be a perfect opportunity to use against the Catholics. But Queen Mary's husband, now King of France proceeded to challenge Elizabeth's claim to the throne on the grounds that she was the illegitimate daughter of Henry VIII and argued that Mary was the rightful Queen of England.

The aphorism that 'truth is stranger than fiction' might easily have stemmed from the life of Mary, Queen of Scots. When she married the heir to France's throne she signed a treaty promising him Scotland if she should die childless. As it turned out, he died first and Scotland was safe in her hands. Or so she said. Although a devout Catholic, when she returned home in 1560 she announced that she had no objection if her subjects preferred to be Protestant, a move no doubt influenced by the fact that John Knox and his followers had, during her absence in France, promulgated a covenant outlawing the Latin Mass in Scotland. They had also negotiated the Treaty of Edinburgh, recognising Elizabeth, and not Mary, as the Queen of England. Most important of all, they had reduced the power of the Queen of Scotland with the establishment of the Kirk of Scotland, governing through Kirk Sessions of lay elders, and eventually through the appointment of Presbyters, who had the power to ordain ministers and settle disputes. The power naturally spilled over into secular matters, and the church, with its own democratic form of government, eventually became more important in the day-to-day life of the country than the monarchy.

For Mary's part, she was willing to work within the system, even if she refused to give up her religion and surrounded herself with Protestant advisors. The fact that the Catholic Mass was part of her daily life, even if it was against the law, scandalized her subjects. They had no idea what scandal was.

Some eyebrows were raised when Mary married her cousin, Henry Stewart, Lord Darnley, a Catholic who seemed to personify the evils the Scots had come to associate with Catholicism. Less than a year into the marriage, she fell in love with David Riccio, her Italian secretary. Darnley put the affair, and Riccio, to an end by murdering him, but the act also brought the marriage to an end. Darnley was later strangled and the building that was the scene of the crime dynamited. Among the suspected perpetrators was James Hepburn, the Earl of Bothwell, who immediately divorced his wife and married the Queen. Although her third marriage was in a Protestant church, the people were not pleased and Mary was forced to abdicate, after which she was imprisoned in a castle on Loch Leven. For his part, Bothwell exiled himself to Norway. The new King of Scotland was Mary's son, James VI, yet another in Scotland's long line of infant monarchs.

Mary managed to escape from her prison and threw herself on the mercy of her cousin, Elizabeth of England, who kept her under house arrest for twenty years before finally having her beheaded in what some people believe was an invented plot against the Queen's life. Young James managed to stay above the battle because he knew it wasn't a good idea to rock England's boat. Elizabeth had no heir, and she wasn't getting any younger.

When the Virgin Queen died in 1603 James's dream came true, and he left immediately for London to become England's King James I. The adjustment was almost too easy, and the monarch became more English than Scottish, suggesting that his job would be much easier if the two kingdoms were merged as one. He began using the term Great Britain to describe his kingdom, calling its flag the Union Jack, and in 1607 a new Act of Union was passed making Scotland and England one

Highland cattle in Keltie Glen, above Callander, Central.

country. But there was no treaty and there was no popular support for one. For their part, the English felt the Scots were too warlike for a peaceful marriage, and north of the border the Presbyterians, who had reason to consider James their enemy, saw the merger as a threat to their independence.

When James's son Charles became king he took it upon himself to bring the Scottish Kirk into the Church of England, a policy he promulgated with his coronation as King of Scotland with full Anglican rites. Then he proposed a new prayer book, based on the English model, to replace the Calvinist belief in spontaneous prayer. It represented the insidious Church of Rome to the Scots, and when the book was formally introduced, rioting broke out in Edinburgh. The riots continued for months, and eventually a new document, known as the National Covenant, calling for support of 'the True Religion', but stopping short of condemning the King, was enthusiastically signed and endorsed by thousands all over Scotland.

Although it was a theological statement, the Covenant was also, in the eyes of most Scots, a declaration of Scottish independence. It was also a signal that war was in the air, and young Scotsmen who had been serving with distinction in armies all over the world began coming home, fully armed, to be in at the beginning when the blood started flowing. Charles, who didn't have an army worthy of the name, sent troops anyway to meet the threat but met a stand-off at Berwick

instead. Not long afterwards, the Scots retaliated with an attack on Newcastle and Durham, and Charles was forced to call a session of the English Parliament. Parliament had not met in ten years, and the session was to give an opportunity for long-held grievances to be aired, creating a power struggle that mushroomed into a civil war.

The Scots supported Oliver Cromwell and his Roundheads in hopes that he would make Presbyterianism the state religion of England and Ireland as well as of Scotland. But when Charles was beheaded by the rebels, the Scots rebelled against Cromwell, who had offended them by murdering a Scottish-born king. They kept the Scottish monarchy alive by crowning Charles II at Edinburgh, but Cromwell's army retaliated by turning Scotland into an occupied country and abolishing its parliament.

After the monarchy was restored in 1660, Charles had stripped the Kirk of most of its power, and violence, rooted in intolerance, gave the name of 'the killing time' to the rest of his reign. During those years secret groups, calling themselves Covenanters, held open air church meetings in defiance of the king, whose successor, James II, made such worship a capital offence. After James was deposed by William of Orange, many in Scotland, especially in the Highlands, remained loyal to the former king and declared war on William. These Jacobites nearly succeeded by defeating William of Orange's forces, but their leaders were killed and enthusiasm for the Jacobite cause

*The Cuillin Hills and Loch
Harport, Isle of Skye,
Highland Region.*

cooled. King William responded by demanding the undivided loyalty of all the clans, and when the leader of Clan MacDonald seemed slow to get the message, he ordered the Campbells to call their old enemies together under a flag of friendship and then to kill all the MacDonalds under the age of seventy. The resulting massacre at Glencoe horrified the Scots, not because so many died, but because the tradition of hospitality had been breached.

Matters got worse when William died and the throne went to Queen Anne, daughter of James II and a Stuart (the spelling of their ancestral name had been changed in the days of Mary, Queen of Scots). None of her children survived, and on her death the English, determined to end the Stuart line, turned to Sophie of Hanover to help them change the line of succession. As a granddaughter of James VI of Scotland and I of England, her blood lines were correct, but succession from then on would be Hanoverian. The English were generous in offering trade concessions in return for Scottish acquiescence, but it was sugar coating for a bitter pill. The English insisted that the two countries unite under a single parliament. Rioting broke out, of course, but in 1707 the inevitable happened. A treaty of Union incorporated the Scottish parliament into the English parliament at Westminster, and Scotland and England became known as the United Kingdom.

Needless to say, it wasn't a red letter day for Scotland, and the eighteenth century was a time of fierce rebellion,

particularly from the Jacobites, who were more convinced than ever that the Stuarts would be their salvation. They had plenty of outside help, first from the French and then the Spanish, but the Jacobites were no match for the English until 1745, when Charles Edward Stuart, known as 'Bonnie Prince Charlie', led them to glory, first establishing his own royal court in Edinburgh and then leading his troops into England itself. His support came from the Highlands, and when he tried to rally southerners to his cause his pleas fell on deaf ears. He was forced to retreat to Drummossie Moor near Inverness, at Culloden, where his army was soundly defeated. It was the last great land battle in Britain, and marked the end of the power of the clans. Charles barely escaped with his life and went into an ignominious exile and most of the Jacobite leaders were executed and their lands confiscated by the Crown.

At the same time, it was made illegal to carry any kind of weapon, from the smallest dirk to the biggest musket, or to wear the traditional tartan, even to play the bagpipes. But, ironically, if the past was being systematically snuffed out, the future was brighter than at any time in Scottish history, thanks to what has been called the Scottish Enlightenment. It was an age of philosophers and poets, of new industrialists and inventors. During the second half of the eighteenth century Scotland's population hardly changed, but its gross national product jumped by as much as fifty per cent. New roads were constructed, new canals built, and what had always been one of

Europe's poorest countries was well on its way to becoming both rich and influential.

The new quest for affluence prompted land owners to improve their holdings but, in the Highlands at least, progress had a down side. Sheep farmers from the south, now with cash in their pockets, began tempting northern landowners with unprecedented rents for their land in the north, which was bringing a meagre return from tenant farming. The problem, of course, was what to do with the farmers. Many were bought out, many simply driven out, in another round of the Highland Clearances that had plagued them since the days of Bonnie Prince Charlie. Some went to the industrialized south where they could get jobs, but an alarming number opted to leave their homeland, never to return.

By the end of the nineteenth century most of Scotland's population was centred in the south, the region that had become an industrial giant. The population had more than quadrupled because of a spurt of immigration by people, chiefly from Ireland, who took advantage of the opportunities a regular paycheque could give them.

The historic rift between Englishmen and Scotsmen began to vanish, too, especially after Queen Victoria began saying nice things about Scotland. She and her consort, Prince Albert, began spending their summers there, and she kept a journal of their idyllic days in the Highlands. 'Oh! what can equal the beauties of nature!', she gushed, adding that 'Albert enjoys it so much. He is in ecstasies here.' After their visit in 1847, the Queen and her consort leased the ancient castle at Balmoral, which they subsequently bought and tore down to make room for a Gothic wedding-cake of a castle in, well, Victorian style. She decorated the place in patterns based on the tartan of the House of Stuart, which she proudly proclaimed to be her own ancestral family. After her beloved Albert died in 1861 she found peace in her grief at Balmoral, and her annual visits began to include railway tours of the Scottish countryside. Her successors have all inherited her enthusiasm for Scotland and the castle still serves as the Royal Family's summer cottage, much to the delight of the Scots, who view the monarch's presence as a symbol that Edinburgh is still their capital, even if for only part of the year.

The union of the two countries was further strengthened by Scotsmen who served, and often died, in the service of an expanding British Empire. Centuries earlier an Englishman had disparagingly remarked that 'the Scots are not industrious and the people are poor. They spend all their time in wars, and when there is no war, they fight each other.' Even though he was wrong about the industriousness of his neighbours, he was quite right about their skills in matters of warfare. Although that was hardly the reason behind the union of England and Scotland, it was fortuitous for the former that Scotland became the first country to be annexed into the British Empire. From that time on Great Britain's destiny depended to an extent on the skills and the unique spirit of the Highland regiments. Their outstanding bravery can be seen by the part that they played in World War I, when 147,000 young Scotsmen died defending the Union Jack. The number represented some twenty percent of the British total, far, far out of proportion to population figures. The numbers were, mercifully, much lower in the Second World War, but the war itself came to Scotland, as it did to England, from the air. Although Glasgow was the most important port in Britain, serving as the port of entry for American and Canadian troops as well as the hub of Britain's shipbuilding industry, it was not attacked until late in 1940. Even then, the air raid was a minor affair, and the German bombers didn't come back again for another six months or so, and the follow-up raids, which ended early in 1943, were puny compared to those further south.

There are war memorials in just about every village in Scotland, and mementoes of wars fought on Scottish soil that seem far out of proportion to a country so small. But if a Scotsman is always ready to try to show that he can beat any man in the house, he is also part of what is easily the most hospitable race on the face of the earth. To millions of people everywhere the Scots have made two great gifts to the world's everlasting pleasure: golf and Scotch whisky. It isn't possible to say which of the gifts is more important. Such judgements are highly individual.

Purists say that golf was actually invented by the Dutch, but the mania for the game clearly began in Scotland where, in the fifteenth century, King James II decided that it was taking his subjects' minds away from serving him. He thought he had nipped the problem in the bud when he issued a decree telling his minions that 'the futeball and golfe be utterly cryed down and not be used'. His words fell on deaf ears, though, and after a century or two even his illustrious offspring had been bitten by the bug. Indeed, it was said that Mary, Queen of Scots nearly missed the funeral of her murdered husband, Darnley, because she was preoccupied with a game of golf.

Even if it is true that they were playing golf in Holland long before the Scots got the idea, it is generally assumed that the game developed in Scotland as an outgrowth of an old habit of walkers who aimlessly knocked pebbles along ahead of them with a stick. It became more purposeful when a Scotsman came up with the idea that a ball made of leather and stuffed with feathers was not only easier to hit but sailed much further and faster than a rock. It wasn't until the middle of the nineteenth century that another Scotsman, a clergyman no less, experimented with a rubber ball filled with liquid latex, and was pleased with how much it improved his score. Although the game had spread around the world by then, it was generally agreed that there was no better place to play it than Scotland. One reason was that there was plenty of land considered too poor for farming, but perfect terrain for chasing a golf ball. Most of the early courses, as well as the best of the modern ones, were along the coast, where wide strips of land were sodden with salt and not much good for any kind of agriculture. Such areas, connecting the seashore with the better land beyond, were called links. The word is still used as a generic term for golf courses, but most of the ones that technically qualify for the name are in the British Isles, and the best of them are in Scotland.

The Scottish tradition from the very beginning was that

golf was a thoroughly democratic game, and laws were passed to secure the rights of even the poorest citizens to tee off even if a nobleman was waiting impatiently to begin his round. In England and other places where land was scarce and expensive, the game was more often restricted to businessmen well-heeled enough to afford the greens fees. The idea came to Scotland in the form of gentlemen's clubs, beginning with the Honourable Company of Edinburgh Golfers, which held the world's first tournament at Leith in 1744. About a century later, King William IV gave his blessing to the St Andrews Society by allowing them to change their name to the Royal and Ancient Golf Club of St Andrews. But for all that, the courses the gentlemen considered their own were pointedly kept open to the public. They still are.

Scotch whisky, which ranks among the top five exports from the British Isles, is one of the few products of any country that can't be duplicated anywhere else, even though many, including the Japanese, have tried. It isn't as though the recipe is complicated or the manufacturing process mysterious. Back in the eighteenth century, even poor and illiterate Highlanders knew how to make it, and millions of gallons of the stuff poured from their stills, making the drink that they called in Gaelic usquebaugh, almost as common as water and certainly more available than milk. Yet, even if everyone knew how to make this 'water of life', there is obviously a secret involved. Most authorities agree that it is a combination of a damp climate, pure soft water and peat, but having said that, their learned discussions usually trail off into a long list of variables as if to prove there really is some kind of secret behind every glass of scotch and that they're not sure what it is. Some will say that the water is perfect because it flows over granite outcroppings into peat bogs. Others agree that the combination of granite and peat is probably nature's best water purifier, but insist that the combination doesn't work unless the water flows from the peat to the granite and not the other way around. The distilling process won't produce anything resembling scotch whisky, many say, unless the barley malt is dried over peat fires, although no one knows for sure why that might be so. Others who have tried to plumb the secret are convinced that it lies in the pure Scottish air that seeps into the oak casks where the whisky is aged for eight years or more. Finally, many say that the difference is in the fact that Scotch whisky is distilled twice, compared to others that are run through just one still. But if that were all it took, they'd be making scotch in France, where the drink is far more popular than cognac, and in the United States, where it beats bourbon as the libation of choice.

If the secret is in age-old distilling methods, a Royal Commission officially decided as far back as 1905 that modern technology was just as effective as any old home-made copper still. After a patent still was developed in 1830, the industry moved out of the cottages and into factories. The new method produced a slightly different, lighter drink, but still unmistakably Scotch, even though veteran drinkers didn't think so. In fact, the old-timers were so upset that they went to court to secure a ruling that the product of the new patent stills couldn't be called whisky at all and should not be sold as such in pubs. After long deliberation, the judges decided that the question was far too weighty for them to answer and turned the problem over to the Royal Commission which, after a great deal of sampling, declared that, while there was a difference, the new product was every bit as good as the old, just lighter. And with that the marketers went to work promoting the lighter, more delicate product. The next logical step was to blend malt and grain whiskies which allowed each brand to claim it was different from, if not better than, all the others. There are more than hundred distilleries in Scotland each making such claims and a lot of them are debatable. One thing that they do all agree on, however, is that if it isn't made in Scotland, it isn't Scotch.

A notable variation on the theme is the liqueur called Drambuie, which its makers say is based on a secret recipe handed down to them from Bonnie Prince Charlie, whose image appears on every bottle, dressed in the tartan of the Stuarts. Or is it? After the Battle of Culloden in 1746, the clans were broken up and for nearly forty years the wearing of traditional highland dress was forbidden. For centuries before then, bright colours in striped and checked designs, called 'setts', had been the standard Highland fashion, but there is no record that any specific designs were used to identify different clans or regional identity. During the years when no one wore them, the old setts were largely forgotten, but when George IV visited Edinburgh in the early nineteenth century dressed in what his tailors considered a traditional Highland outfit, it became one of the most far-reaching fashion statements of all time. Overnight, new setts were created and given family names, more often than not with no historical connection to the ancient clans, and most often with no serious research into traditional designs, if indeed such designs had ever had any significance. Nothing is safe from the designs, which are featured on all manner of goods, from boxes of shortbread to shoes, tea towels, raincoats and even whisky bottles. And even if your name has no Scottish lilt to it, there is probably a marketer somewhere calling himself a genealogist who can provide your family tartan made up into any number of products that will allow you to show your very own colours.

And why not? Pride runs strong in Scotland, and the Scots are eager to share their heritage with you. They don't mind a bit if your real roots are elsewhere.

*Above: Caerlaverock
Castle, Dumfries and
Galloway.*

*Above: Jedburgh Abbey,
Borders.*

Imposing and detailed arches, flying buttresses and towers, all wrought in red sandstone, are typical of Borders ruined abbeys. Caerlaverock Castle was first built in 1220 and has had a stormy history. Jedburgh Abbey, founded 1118 is noted for its fine nave. The Cistercian Melrose Abbey, Scotland's best known ruined abbey, was founded in 1136, and it is said that the heart of Robert Bruce was buried under the chancel's east window. Pilgrims come in their thousands to visit Dryburgh Abbey, founded in 1150, as it is the burial place of Sir Walter Scott and Field-Marshall Earl Haig.

Above: Dryburgh Abbey,
Borders.

*Below: Abbotsford House,
near Melrose, Borders.*

Abbotsford House, near Melrose, Borders, was the last and most famous of Sir Walter Scott's homes and stands near his beloved River Tweed. The house and its gardens were largely designed by Scott. Scott's View is the name given to a point east of Melrose favoured by Scott for its beautiful view over the Tweed towards the Eildon Hills, an important Borders landmark. The Borders town of Kelso is best known for its ruined abbey, founded in 1128. The abbey still displays some fine Norman and early Gothic details.

*Above: From Scott's View,
near the Eildon Hills,
Borders.*

*Below: Kelso Abbey ruins,
Borders.*

*Overleaf: The Eildon Hills from
Scott's View.*

St Abb's is a small and picturesque resort and fishing village on the Borders coast. It is backed by red sandstone cliffs which rise to over 300 feet in height and are dotted with ancient smugglers' caves. The rugged St Abb's Head cliffs, topped with a lighthouse, can be best viewed from the inlet of Pettycarwick Bay.

Left: St Abb's harbour, Borders.

*Above: Dunbar harbour,
Lothian.*

Dunbar, situated on the east coast of
Lothian, is a historical fishing port. The
ruined castle, perched on a rock
overlooking the harbour, was destroyed
soon after the fall of Mary Queen of·
Scots in 1568. The red of the castle
walls is echoed in the rich, red local soil
which produces the famous Dunbar Red
potato. North-west from Dunbar along
the Lothian coast towards North
Berwick stands the 14th-century
Tantallon Castle, besieged and ruined in
1651. These ruins overlook the mighty
350-foot high Bass Rock. This was once
the site of a Covenanters' prison, but is
now home only to a lighthouse and
many sea birds.

Below: The harbour and castle, Dunbar, Lothian.

Above: Tantallon Castle and Bass Rock, Lothian.

Below: Edinburgh from Calton Hill.

Above: Scott Monument, Princes Street, Edinburgh.

Scotland's capital, Edinburgh, was built on a collection of hills. Between Calton Hill and Castle Hill is elegant Princes Street, the city's main artery. The street was named after George III's sons. The Scott Monument, dedicated to Sir Walter Scott and fashioned by George Kemp between the years 1840 and 1844, stands in Princes Street Gardens. Charles Cockerell's Parthenon tops Calton Hill. A castle has stood on Edinburgh's Castle Hill for at least 1,000 years. Each weekday at 1300 hours a gun is fired from the Castle as a time check.

Above: Princes Street, Edinburgh.

Overleaf: Fireworks at Edinburgh Castle.

Below: Edinburgh Castle from Princes Street Gardens.

Edinburgh Castle sits magnificently on Castle Rock, overlooking Princes Street, Princes Street Gardens and the Old Town. Holyrood Palace, situated at the eastern end of Edinburgh's Royal Mile, is the Queen's official residence when in Scotland. It was founded by James IV in 1550 around a 13th-century abbey. Most of the building and interior was commissioned by Charles II. Mary Queen of Scots lived here 1561-1567, and it was here that she married Bothwell, following the death of Darnley.

Above:Holyrood Palace, Edinburgh.

Above: Pittenweem, Fife.

*Overleaf: Firth of Forth
rail bridge at sunset.*

The ancient fishing communities of Pittenweem and Cellardyke lie to either side of Anstruther, a Fife fishing village known for its herring catch. Sir Benjamin Baker built the cantilevered Firth of Forth rail bridge between 1883 and 1890 at an ancient ferry point - North and South Queensferry - on the Firth of Forth near Dunfermline. The railway bridge is considered one of the finest engineering feats in the world. It is 2,765 yards long and rests upon Inchgarvie Island which lies in the firth.

Below: Firth of Forth rail bridge from North Queensferry.

Above: Cellardyke harbour, near Anstruther, Fife.

Below: Falkland Palace, Fife.

Above: St Andrews Old Course Club House, Fife.

Falkland Palace in the picturesque cobbled Royal Burgh of Falkland was a favourite royal seat from the time of James V. His daughter, the future Mary Queen of Scots, used to hunt from this palace. The royal tennis courts of 1539 are still kept up. South of Falkland lie the Lomond Hills with their remarkable wind eroded structures like the 'Bannet Stane' or Bonnet Stone near Strathmiglo. St Andrews' famous golf courses lie to the north-west of the historic Fife town. The Old Course is the world's oldest golf course, dating back to the 15th century.

Above: The Bonnet Stone, Lomond Hills, Fife.

*Below: Stirling Castle,
Central.*

*Above: Burns Monument,
Stirling, Central.*

Stirling, built on a meander on the River
Forth, was known as the Gateway to the
North as it was the last crossing point from
the south to the Highlands. The original
old bridge is still used by pedestrians.
Stirling Castle is magnificently situated on
a 250-foot high rock overlooking the
battlefield of Bannockburn. Callandar,
north-west of Stirling is situated where the
Teith and Leni rivers meet. The town is
overlooked from the north-west by Ben
Ledi which rises to 2,875 feet. This is a
popular area among climbers and hill
walkers. Bridge of Allan, directly to the
north of Stirling, looks to the north-east
onto the Ochil Hills.

*Above: Callander, backed
by Ben Ledi, Central.*

*Overleaf: Ochil Hills,
Central.*

*Below: Loch Ard and Ben
Lomond at Aberfoyle,
Central.*

*Above: Loch Venachar
and Ben Venue,
Trossachs, Central.*

Aberfoyle, a village east of Loch
Ard, is known as the Gateway to
the Trossachs – the hills to the
north. The well-known Duke's
Road, built in the 19th century,
leads due north from Aberfoyle to
the Trossachs, and from this road
there are fine views of Loch
Venachar. Loch Ard Forest reaches
to east and west from Aberfoyle
and forms part of the Forestry
Commission's Queen Elizabeth
Forest Park. Loch Lubnaig lies
northeast of Aberfoyle and the
Trossachs.

*Above: Loch Lubnaig and
Ardnandave Hill, Central.*

Above: Loch Iubhair and Ben Imirean, Glen Dochart, Central.

Overleaf: Strath Fillan Water, Ben More and Stobinian, Central.

Crianlarich is a centre for climbing and walking. It lies at the meeting of Strath Fillan, Glen Dochart and Glen Falloch. Beyond Loch Dochart is Loch Iubhair in whose waters the twin peaks of Ben More and Stobinian are reflected to the south. To the north rises Ben Imirean. Tyndrum at the north-west end of Strath Fillan, is popular with anglers and climbers. Nearby is the splendid peak of Ben Lui on whose slopes rises Strath Fillan Water, which later becomes known as the Dochart, and later still as the Tay.

Below: Strath Fillan Water and Ben More, Criancarich, Central.

Above: Ben Lui, near Tyndrum, Central.

The Trossachs literally means 'bristly country'. It is a lovely area of mountains, lochs and rivers that stretches along a thickly wooded gorge connecting Loch Achray to Loch Katrine, Central.

Left: Loch Achray, Central.

Inversnaid, which lies due west of the Trossachs, is situated on the east bank of Loch Lomond. It is surrounded by splendid mountains whose rivers and waterfalls feed the loch. Loch Katrine is the most famous loch of the Trossachs area, eulogised by Sir Walter Scott in his poem *Lady of the Lake*. There is no public road around the loch, and the best way to admire the fine rugged scenery is to take a steamer such as the S.S. Sir Walter Scott which leaves from the pier at Stronachlachar. There is a pass between Loch Katrine and Loch Achray, in the direction of Ben A'an which is known as Duke's Pass.

Above: Waterfall at Inversnaid, Central.

Overleaf: Loch Katrine from Ben A'an, Central.

Below: Stronachlachar
Loch Katrine, Central.

Above: Duke's Pass at
Loch Katrine, Central.

Tarbet lies on a narrow neck of land that connects the western shore of Loch Lomond to the north-eastern shore of Loch Long. There are fantastic views of Loch Lomond - 'The Queen of Scottish Lakes' - and of Ben Lomond (3,192 feet) from this village. The famous song about Loch Lomond, Britain's largest lake is said to have been composed by a captured follower of Bonny Prince Charlie on the eve of his execution. In the song he says his spirit will return to his homeland along the 'low road' after death, quicker than his friend travelling along the 'high road'.

Left: Tarbet, Loch Lomond, Strathclyde.

Overleaf: Loch Lomond and Ben Lomond, Strathclyde.

*Below: Loch Lomond and
Ben Lomond, Strathclyde.*

*Above: Loch Lomond and
Ben Lomond from Duck
Bay, Strathclyde.*

Ben Lomond, which stands at 3,192 feet, dominates Loch Lomond, Britain's largest lake, and is snow-clad throughout the winter months. It is also one of the main scenic features to be seen from Loch Long and the village of Arrocher, situated only 2 miles from the western shore of Loch Lomond. Further north on the western shore of Loch Lomond is the site of the Loch Sloy hydroelectric power station at Inveruglas, from where there are also wonderful views to be had of this fine lake.

Above: Loch Long, Arrocher and Ben Lomond, Strathclyde.

Overleaf: Loch Lomond and Ben Lomond from Inveruglas, Strathclyde.

Below: Rhu Marina, Firth of Clyde, Strathclyde.

Above: The Turnberry Golf Hotel, Turnberry, Strathclyde.

Below: Burns Monument,
Alloway, Strathclyde.

The village of Rhu with its popular yachting marina faces southwards across the River Clyde onto the important industrial centres of Greenock and Port Glasgow. Greenock is the birthplace of James Watt, inventor of the steam engine, who was born here in 1736. Alloway, further south down the Strathclyde coast just south of Ayr, is the birthplace of Scotland's national poet Robert Burns who was born 25th January 1759, a date celebrated annually as Burn's Night. Turnberry, situated still further south down the Strathclyde west coast on Turnberry Bay, is famous for its golf course. From this course golfers can gaze across the Firth of Clyde onto the mountains of the Island of Arran.

Overleaf: Greenock on the
River Clyde, Strathclyde.

69

Below: Tarbert harbour,
Loch Fyne, Strathclyde.

Tarbert and Inveraray are at opposite ends of Loch Fyne. Tarbert, down at the far southern end, is the centre of the Loch Fyne herring industry and lies on an isthmus of land dividing Loch Fyne from West Loch Tarbert. Inveraray is a beautiful whitewashed Royal Burgh on the northwest shores of Loch Fyne. It is surrounded by lovely woodlands, and its castle is the seat of the Clan Campbell. The castle has a magnificent interior and houses some valuable portraits. The end of Robert Louis Stevenson's novel *Catriona* describes the Inveraray area.

Above: Inveraray, Loch
Fyne, Strathclyde.

Below: Inveraray Castle, Strathclyde.

Overleaf: Inveraray Castle on Loch Fyne, Strathclyde.

Kyles of Bute is a beautiful
horseshoe-shaped strait of water
separating the Scottish mainland
from Bute. It is a popular area for
yachting regattas. Tighnabruaich is
a Gaelic word meaning House on
the Brae, referring to the one house
that used to stand at this point
above Kyles of Bute looking over
the strait onto the island. It is now
a resort favoured by yachting
enthusiasts, and has a steamer pier
serving the island.

Right: Kyles of Bute,
Tighnabruaich,
Strathclyde.

Overleaf: Firth of Clyde
and Kyles of Bute,
Strathclyde.

Above: Ben More, Isle of Mull, Strathclyde.

The Isle of Mull is the largest of the Inner Hebridean islands. Tobermory is Mull's main centre and fishing port. The island is wild and rugged and its highest point, Ben More, stands at 3,169 feet. A ferry links Fionphort on the far west coast of Mull with the tiny island of Iona. Iona is famous for its cathedral and associations with St Columba who brought Christianity to Scotland from Ireland in AD 563. The cathedral was founded in the 13th century, but the present building dates from the 15th century. The adjoining buildings, which have undergone restoration, comprise the original monastery's chapter house, refectory, undercroft and cloister. The Isle of Tiree, which lies north-west of Mull and Iona, is flat and fertile and mainly devoted to crofting.

Overleaf: Tobermory, Isle of Mull, Strathclyde.

*Below: Iona Cathedral,
Iona, Strathclyde.*

*Above: Scarinish harbour,
Isle of Tiree, Strathclyde.*

Oban, a famous Strathclyde resort, hosts the West Highland Yachting Week in August and the Argyll Gathering in September. It is popular for golf and for taking ferry trips to the nearby islands of Mull, Lismore, Iona and Staffa. McCaig's Folly, which sits on a hill overlooking the town of Oban, is an uncompleted copy of Rome's Coliseum. It was financed by a banker to ease unemployment during the late 19th century, and was to be a museum and art gallery. It has walls 2 feet thick and up to 47 feet high, and the courtyard inside has now been landscaped. It is floodlit at night.

Right: McCaig's Folly above Oban, Strathclyde.

*Below: Near Dalmally by
the River Orchy,
Strathclyde.*

Dalmally is located on the south bank of the River Orchy near to where it flows into Loch Awe, west of the village. Mighty Kilchurn Castle, founded in 1440 by the Bredalbane family is situated nearby. Ben Cruachan makes an imposing backdrop to the castle and loch. North-west of Loch Awe and north of Oban is Loch Linnhe and the Appin area, where the rather bleak Castle Stalker can be seen perched on its rock. This region was described by Robert Louis Stevenson in his novel Kidnapped. Inveroran, inland from Strathclyde's rugged western coast, looks across Loch Tulla onto the Black Mount and its peak, Stob Ghabhar which is 3,565 feet in height.

*Above: Castle Stalker near
Appin, Strathclyde.*

STRATHCLYDE

Below: Kilchurn Castle, Loch Awe, Strathclyde.

Overleaf: Loch Tulla and Stob Ghabhar, Strathclyde.

87

*Below: Scone Palace,
near Perth, Tayside.*

*Above: Glamis Castle,
Tayside.*

Above: Drummond Castle, near Crieff, Tayside.

Scone Palace lies to the north of Perth. All the early Scottish kings were crowned at Scone Abbey on this site. Charles II was the last king to be crowned here in 1651. The present palace was built between 1803 and 1808. Glamis Castle lies due north of Dundee and was probably the setting for Shakespeare's Macbeth. The oldest parts of the castle date from the 14th century, but much of it was rebuilt in the 17th century in the style of a French chateau. Drummond Castle, near Crieff, was originally built by the 1st Lord Drummond in 1491, though only the square tower remains from this time.

Below: Loch Tay, Tayside.

*Above: Oil rape fields near
Perth, Tayside.*

Below: Autumnal beech tree, Tayside.

Tayside is an area of peace and great unspoilt natural beauty. Loch Tay has the richest salmon fishing waters in Britain. Agricultural land is very productive and there are rivers and many areas of forest. From Hermitage Bridge, south of Dunkeld, there are fine views of the River Bran and its falls.

Overleaf: River Bran, near Dunkeld, Tayside.

Below: Autumn in Glen Lyon, Tayside.

Glen Lyon is one of the loveliest and longest glens in Scotland. The meaning of glen is 'narrow valley' and this one runs for 25 miles, north of Loch Tay in the Breadalbane country. The glen is approached through the richly wooded Pass of Lyon. The River Lyon joins the River Tay just east of Loch Tay. There is thought to have been a Roman outpost in this area.

Above: Roman bridge in Glen Lyon, Tayside.

Below: Ben Vrackie over-looking Loch Faskally, Pitlochry, Tayside.

Pitlochry is a centre from which to visit the Grampian mountains and in summer hosts the Pitlochry Theatre Festival. Sometimes Pitlochry is said to be the exact centre of Scotland. Ben Vrackie , which stands at 2,757 feet, looks down on the town. Loch Fascally was created as a result of the 54-foot Pitlochry Dam, constructed on the River Tummel to the west of the town as part of an extensive hydroelectric power development. Just north of Pitlochry is the Pass of Killiecrankie which is overlooked by Ben a'Ghlo.

Below: Pass of Killiecrankie, Tayside.

Above: Loch Dunmore, Pitlochry, Tayside.

Below: Tummel Valley,
Pitlochry, Tayside.

Above: Tummel Valley and
Ben a'Ghlo, Tayside.

Below: Tummel Valley and Ben Vrackie, Tayside.

The River Tummel flows through a peaceful wooded valley, overlooked by dark, rounded peaks such as Ben Vrackie (2,757 feet) and Ben a'Ghlo (3,505 feet). Glen Fincastle leads into the Tummel Valley north-west of Pitlochry, which is well-known for its hydroelectric power development and its summer theatre festival.

Overleaf: Ben Vrackie, Tayside.

Below: Schiehallion by
Loch Rannoch, Tayside.

Overleaf: Loch Tummel
and Schiehallion from
Queen's View, Tayside.

Below: Loch Tummel, Tayside.

Waters from Loch Rannoch flow eastwards into the River Tummel, and then into a reservoir that is part of an extensive hydroelectric scheme, and then into Loch Tummel. The area is surrounded by forests and moorland, and is home to the distinctive conical quartzite peak of Schiehallion, one of the best-known landmarks of the central highlands. Queen's View is a famous viewing point over Loch Tummel which was named after Queen Victoria's visit to the spot in 1866. It is on the north bank of the River Tummel just east of the Loch. The Schiehallion peak dominates the view.

Above: Loch Tummel, Tayside.

Above: Blair Castle, Blair Atholl, Tayside.

Overleaf: Blair Castle, Blair Atholl, Tayside.

The Duke of Atholl built Blair Castle in 1269 at this meeting point of several glens, magnificently backed by the Grampian mountains. Lying just north of Pitlochry, the castle has been renovated and restored over the years in the Scottish baronial style. The oldest part is Cumming's Tower, built in the 13th century. Blair Castle holds a valuable collection of furniture. The castle is the seat of the Duke of Atholl who is head of the Clan Murray. He is the only Briton permitted to maintain a private army, which is named the Atholl Highlanders.

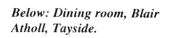

Below: Dining room, Blair Atholl, Tayside.

Above: Drawing room, Blair Castle, Tayside.

Below: Crathes Castle, near Banchory, Grampian.

Crathes Castle lies between Aberdeen and Banchory just to the north of the River Dee. It dates from the 16th century and has some fine painted ceilings and woodwork. It stands in 575 acres and boasts one of the best collections of trees and shrubs in Britain. The ruins of the 16th-century Edzell Castle lie in Tayside, close to the border with Grampian. Its Stirling tower still stands, as does a bower once used by Mary Queen of Scots. The lovely walled garden was laid out by Lord Edzell in 1604. The Royal Burgh of Elgin is best known for its cathedral ruins which date from 1224. This great ecclesiastical building, once known as the Lantern of the North, suffered fire and other damage over the centuries, but there is still much original work preserved, such as the choir. Also of interest are the founder's grave and other ancient tombs and their inscriptions.

Above: Edzell Castle, Tayside.

Below: Elgin Cathedral, Grampian.

Below: Old Bridge of Dee,
Royal Deeside, Grampian.

Above: Crathie Church,
Royal Deeside. Grampian.

Royal Deeside is the area between the resorts of Ballater and Braemar and includes the royal castle of Balmoral. Queen Victoria, who visited and popularised the area, laid the foundation stone of Crathie Church in 1895. It is here that the Royal Family worship when in residence at Balmoral. The Dee is a fine salmon river which flows through beautiful forested and heather-clad hills. Its upper reaches to the west of Braemar are particularly fast and wild. Clunie Water flows into the River Dee in the north of the village of Braemar, and this separates the village into two districts, namely, Castleton of Braemar and Auchindryne. Three miles to the east of the village is the Old Bridge of Dee, which was built in 1753.

Above: Clunie Water, Braemar, Royal Deeside, Grampian.

Braemar Castle, which dates from
1628, lies just to the north of the
village of Braemar overlooking the
Dee. It was largely rebuilt in 1748
following attack and fire. The area
is dominated by the stunning
heather-clad Cairngorm mountains.
Quoich Water flows from the
Cairngorms down into the Dee just
west of Braemar.

*Right: Braemar Castle,
River Dee, Grampian.*

*Overleaf: River Dee and
Quoich Water, Grampian.*

Below: Inverness Castle,
Highland Region.

Known as the capital of the Highlands, Inverness is one of Scotland's great historic towns. Its castle has been built in modern times, as the original was destroyed in 1746. Cawdor Castle, north-east of Inverness on the River Nairn, is a picturesque and historically important medieval building with a tower dating from 1454, and an original drawbridge and gateway. It is surrounded by lovely gardens. Shakespeare's Macbeth was Thane of Cawdor, and it is here that Duncan is said to have been murdered. The fairy tale Dunrobin Castle looks east out over the North Sea north of the Dornoch Firth. It was founded in 1275, but had extensive additions in 1856. It was the seat of the Duke of Sutherland before becoming a boys' public school.

Above: Cawdor Castle,
Highland Region.

*Below: Dunrobin Castle,
Highland Region.*

Below: Loch Laggan backed by Creag Meaghaidh, Highland Region.

The waters from Loch Laggan run into the River Spey. This loch is overlooked by a range of mountains which are consistently over 3,000 feet for over 10 miles, the highest crag of which is Creag Meaghaidh. The River Spey is the second longest in Scotland and well known for its good salmon fishing. Ben Alder (3,757 feet) rises at the far western end of Loch Ericht, a remote 15-mile long loch that has been harnessed for a hydroelectric power scheme. At the other end of the loch lies the town of Dalwhinnie, on the road linking Perth with Inverness.

*Below: Loch Ericht and
Ben Alder, Highland
Region.*

*Above: Spey Valley,
Highland Region.*

Below: Falls by Loch Laggan, Highland Region.

Above: Loch Arkaig, Highland Region.

Waters from Loch Laggan run into the River Spey, the second longest river in Scotland. The richly wooded slopes of the hills surrounding Loch Arkaig, to the west of Loch Laggan, descend right to the water's edge and encircle this most peaceful and serene highland lake. This area is known as the Great Glen. Lochaber is a Highland district of great beauty stretching from the Great Glen and Loch Levan to Glen Spean and Loch Lochy. Spean Bridge, a village in this district, is on the River Spean which runs into Loch Lochy. The bridge from which the village gets its name was built by Telford in 1819. The Commando Memorial in Spean Bridge was built by Scott Sutherland in 1952 as a memorial to those commandos who trained in this district during the Second World War.

Above: The Commando Memorial, Spean Bridge, Highland Region.

*Below: Caledonian Canal
and Ben Nevis, Lochaber,
Highland Region.*

The Caledonian Canal, which was begun in 1803, runs through the heart of Scotland connecting Inverness with Fort William. The canal enabled sailing vessels to pass from the North Sea to the Atlantic without having to brave the wild Cape Wrath. The canal is linked by Loch Ness, Loch Oich and Loch Lochy. Nowadays it is used mainly for pleasure craft, and not for industrial vessels. It is over 60 miles long and has 29 locks, a series of which are known as Neptune's Staircase near Corpach. Fort Augustus on the south-western extremity of Loch Ness marks the point at which the Caledonian Canal joins the loch. Ruins of Urquhart Castle, which was built during the 13th-16th centuries, are situated on the north bank of Loch Ness overlooking Urquhart Bay. The castle was blown up in 1692 to prevent the Jacobites taking it over.

*Above: Urquhart Castle,
Loch Ness, Highland Region.*

*Above: Caledonian Canal,
Highland Region.*

Below: Skiing on the summit of Aonach Mor, Highland Region.

Above: Skiing in Glencoe, Highland Region.

Below: Skiing at Aonach Mor, Highland Region.

There is snow on Ben Nevis (4,406 feet), Britain's highest mountain, for most of the year.
Skiing is provided for on Aonach Mor (3,999 feet) near Fort William, and in the Happy Valley area of Glencoe. It was at Glencoe that the infamous massacre in 1692 of Macdonalds by the Campbell clan took place.

Overleaf: Aonach Mor towards Carn Mor Dearg and Ben Nevis, Highland Region.

Glencoe is a pass through this spectacular area of Highland mountains that stretches from Loch Leven to the Moor of Rannoch. Glencoe has a bloody history, but more important nowadays a stunning situation, being surrounded by magnificent craggy peaks. On the south side of the glen are the Three Sisters of Glencoe, known as Beinn Fhada, Gearr Aonach and Aonach Dubh which are all between 2,500 feet and 3,000 feet. To the east of Glencoe there is the wild Moor of Rannoch above which rises the peak of Buachaille Etive Mor.

Above: Rannoch Moor and Buachaille Etive Mor, Highland Region.

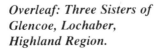

Overleaf: Three Sisters of Glencoe, Lochaber, Highland Region.

Below: Buachaille Etive Mor overlooking Rannoch Moor, Highland Region.

*Above: Glen Etive,
Highland Region.*

*Overleaf: Bishops Bay,
Loch Leven, Highland
Region.*

Lonely Glen Etive, surrounded by
its towering peaks, lies to the east
of Glencoe. On the north side of
the Glencoe ridge, the conical Pap
of Glencoe (2,430 feet) is reflected
in the waters of Loch Leven. From
this loch the Mamore Forest
mountains stretch north-east into
the Lochaber area. Ballachulish, at
the western end of Loch Leven, is
the main village of the Glencoe
area, and behind this rises Ben Vair
with its two 3,000-foot peaks.

Below: Ben Vair, near Ballachulish, Highland Region.

Above: Loch Leven, Pap of Glencoe, Highland Region.

Below: Viaduct in Glenfinnan, Highland Region.

Glenfinnan leads down to the far northern end of Loch Shiel, one of the most beautiful areas of Highland Scotland. It is here at the head of the loch that the Prince Charles Edward tower, topped with its kilted Highlander, was erected in 1815. It was built to commemorate the Highlanders who followed the Prince and raised the royal standard here in 1745. The waters of Loch Ailort flow into the sea opposite the islands of Muck and Eigg.

Above: Prince Charles Edward monument, Glenfinnan, Loch Shiel, Highland Region.

Below: Waterfall into Loch Ailort, Highland Region.

*Below: Mallaig harbour,
Highland Region.*

Mallaig on the west Highland coast, facing Skye, is a fishing port and stopping place for steamers and motor launches to the Hebridean islands. The famous white sands of Morar, facing the islands of Eigg and Rhum, line the bay formed by the Morar River estuary. A little further southwards down this rocky western coast Loch Ailort issues into the sea, opposite the Inner Hebridean Isle of Muck.

Above: White sands of Morar, near Mallaig, Highland Region.

Overleaf: Sunset from Loch Ailort, looking onto Isles Eigg and Rhum, Highland Region.

The Isle of Skye is thought by many to be the most beautiful of all the Scottish islands. It has a very craggy and deeply indented coastline that has been carved into by many sea lochs. Neist Point is the most westerly crag of the island, looking out over Little Minch and the Outer Hebrides. One of Skye's most easterly points is Kyleakin, named after an early Norwegian king. This is a ferry port serving Kyle of Lochalsh. Perched above Kyleakin harbour stand the ruins of Castle Moil. This served as a lookout point to guard against Nordic invaders. The spectacular scenery and rough surface of Skye's Cuillin Hills, to the southwest of the island, provide a rock climber's paradise.

Above: Neist lighthouse, Isle of Skye, Highland Region.

Overleaf: The Cuillin Hills from Glen Sligachan, Isle of Skye, Highland Region.

Below: Sunset over Neist Point,
Isle of Skye, Highland Region.

Above: Castle Moil over Kyleakin harbour,
Isle of Skye, Highland Region.

Dornie lies at the sea end of Loch Duich where it joins Loch Long, just across the water from Skye. Its castle of Eilean Donan, on its pretty off-shore island, was built in 1220 by Alexander II. It was originally completely cut off from the mainland, but is now linked by a little bridge and causeway.

Left: Eilean Donan Castle, Loch Duich, Dornie, Highland Region.

Glen Shiel rivals Glencoe with its wild beauty. Loch Duich, a lovely mountain-encircled sea loch in Glen Shiel, stretches from Shiel Bridge in the south to Dornie in the north. The dominant feature of this loch is the magnificent view to the south-east of the Five Sisters of Kintail, the highest of which is Scour Ouran (3,505 feet).

Above: Highland burn in Glen Shiel.

Overleaf: Loch Duich at Shiel Bridge, Highland Region.

*Below: Dawn over Loch
Duich and Kintail moun-
tains, Highland Region.*

*Above: Loch Duich and
the Five Sisters of Kintail,
Highland Region.*

Above: Plockton, on Loch Carron, Highland Region.

Overleaf: Sunset over Loch Shieldaig, Highland Region.

An idyll of Highland life, the Plockton community live in whitewashed cottages encircling a sheltered inlet on Loch Carron, facing the wild Applecross and Torridon mountains to the north. Wester Ross is the name given to this hilly western half of what was once the county of Ross and Cromarty. It encompasses some of the best Highland scenery including the beautiful red sandstone Torridon mountains, one of whose peaks is Beinn Damh (2,958 feet). Shieldaig on Loch Shieldaig which runs into the sea loch of Torridon just east of Skye, is another spectacular whitewashed village.

Below: Loch an Loin,
backed by Beinn Damh,
Highland Region.

Above: Shieldaig Village
on Loch Shieldaig,
Highland Region.

Wester Ross has many beautifully situated sea lochs which provide excellent swimming and fishing. Sandy Gairloch, on Gair Loch, and Ullapool, on Loch Broom backed by Beinn Ghobhlach (2,082 feet), are two fine examples. To the north of Loch Broom lies the remote and magical Loch Lurgain, behind which rises Cul Beag (2,523 feet). Elphin lies still further north in Wester Ross, backed by Cul More (2,786 feet).

Above: Gairloch sands, Gair Loch, Highland Region.

Overleaf: Ullapool, Loch Broom and Ben Ghobhlach, Highland Region.

Below: Red sandstone rocks backed by Cul Beag, Highland Region.

Above: Culmore and village of Elphin, Highland Region.

*Below: Achmelvich Bay,
Highland Region.*

To the southeast of Lochinver in
the Torridon mountains rise the
peaks of Canisp (2,779 feet) and
Suilven (2,399 feet). The latter is
sometimes called the Sugar Loaf or
Matterhorn of Scotland and has a
mile-and-a-half long ridge. North-
west of Lochinver, facing across
the Minch towards the Western
Isles is the lovely sandy Bay of
Achmelvich, and a little further
north juts the rocky promontory of
the Point of Stoer, above which a
fine lighthouse flashes its warning
beam. Loch Stack lies still further
north in these wild Highland
reaches of north-western Scotland,
and looks onto the peak of Arkle
(2,580 feet).

*Above: Canisp and
Suilven, near Lochinver,
Highland Region.*

Below: Stoer Point light-house, Highland Region.

Overleaf: Loch Stack and Arkle, Highland Region.

*Below: Sango Bay,
Durness, Highland
Region.*

The fine sandy bays of Scotland's
'flat head' with their bold rocks
and promontories, facing not much
more than the Arctic, form a
special and secret part of the world.
Durness, on Sango Bay, is the
nearest place to the treacherous
Cape Wrath. East of this bay, Loch
Eriboll emerges into the sea
backed by the cliffs of Whiten
Head. The Kyle of Tongue is one
of the many straits of water carving
deeply into this rocky northern
coast. Bettyhill on Torrisdale Bay
is popular for its wide expanse of
wave-beaten sands.

*Overleaf: Sango Bay and
Whiten Head, Highland
Region.*

*Below: Kyle of Tongue,
Highland Region.*

*Above: Torrisdale Bay, Bettyhill,
Highland Region.*

Below: The Haven, Sarclet Head, Highland Region.

Below: Stacks of Duncansby, off John o' Groats, Highland Region.

Duncanby Head with its sharks' teeth sea stacks is Scotland's most north-easterly tip. The nearest village is John o' Groats, 873 miles away from the most southerly tip of the British mainland, Land's End in Cornwall. Sarclet Head is situated on the east Highland coast whilst Dornoch Firth is further south down this east coast. Scotland's last execution for witchcraft took place in Dornoch in 1722.

Overleaf: Dornoch Firth, Highland Region.

Below: St Clement's Church, Rodel, Harris, Western Isles.

Above: Castle Bay and Kishmul Castle, Isle of Barra, Western Isles.

The Western Isles are made up of a
130-mile stretch of islands. The
main islands are called Lewis,
Harris, North and South Uist,
Benbecula and Barra. They are
connected to each other by ferries
and causeways. The islands are
buffeted by Atlantic storms which
has led to much erosion and thin
soils. Many of these islanders
speak Gaelic. St Clement's Church
in Rodel, at the far southern end of
Harris, was built in 1500 and
overlooks the Little Minch and the
Sound of Harris. Kishmul Castle
on its tiny island in Castle Bay,
Barra, was built around 1030 for a
pirate chief. Baleshare is another
tiny island, just off North Uist.

*Above: Croft in Baleshare,
North Uist, Western Isles.*

Harris, in the Western Isles, is world famous for its Harris Tweed cloth which is still made on this remote island. Harris is connected by a neck of land to Lewis, and is largely made up of rocky inlets and sandy bays. Barra is the southernmost and smallest of the principal Western Isles. Ersary is on its eastern coast.

Above: Seilbost, Isle of Harris, Western Isles.

Overleaf: Ersary, Isle of Barra, Western Isles.

Below: Husinish Bay, Isle of Harris, Western Isles.

Below: Archaeological remains, Jarlshof, Shetland.

Shetland consists of around 100 islands, only 20 of which are inhabited. They lie north-east of the Orkney Islands and comprise the very most northern of Scotland's islands, and the most northerly part of the United Kingdom. Jarlshof, at the southern tip of the islands, is famous for its very important archaeological remains from the bronze, iron-age and Viking periods. At Esha Ness, lying on the Mainland to the north of St Magnus Bay, wind and wave erosion has resulted in some amazing sea stacks. The bay is said to be good for trout fishing. Lerwick is the capital of this island and harbours fishing vessels from many different countries. Lerwick harbour lies actually just half a mile off Mainland on the opposite island of Bressay.

Above: Archaeological remains, Jarlshof, Shetland.

*Below: Esha Ness,
Shetland.*

*Above: Lerwick harbour,
Bressay, Shetland.*

Below: St Magnus'
Cathedral, Kirkwall,
Orkney.

The Orkney Islands lie 20 miles to the north of the Scottish mainland. The capital, Kirkwall, is home of St Magnus's Cathedral. Splendid in its red and yellow sandstone, this cathedral was founded in 1137. Italian Second World War prisoners made an ornate chapel in one of the Nissen huts on Lamb Holm, a little island between Orkney Mainland and South Ronaldsay.

Above: Italian chapel,
Lamb Holm, Orkney.

Below: Skara Brae, Orkney.

Overleaf: Ring of Brodgar, Orkney.

Last page: Kitchener Memorial on Marwick Head, Orkney.

Below: Yescanaby coast, Orkney.

Skara Brae is on the west coast of the Orkney Mainland, and is the remains of a remarkably well preserved Stone Age settlement from 2,000-2,500 BC. The one-roomed houses contain stone beds, cupboards and fireplaces. Nearby, stand the 20 prehistoric upright stones of the Ring of Brodgar, which are surrounded by a ditch. More standing pillars, this time in the sea and wrought by nature and not by prehistoric man, can be seen at Yescanaby, also on the west coast of Orkney Mainland. A little further north stands the Kitchener Memorial, on the cliffs at Marwick Head. This is near the site of the sinking in 1916 of the cruiser on which General Kitchener was being taken to Russia.

Above: Yescanaby coast, Orkney.